DISCOURAGING TERRORISM

Some Implications of 9/11

Panel on Understanding Terrorists in Order to Deter Terrorism

Neil J. Smelser and Faith Mitchell, *Editors*

Center for Social and Economic Studies

Division of Behavioral and Social Sciences and Education

NATIONAL RESEARCH COUNCIL
OF THE NATIONAL ACADEMIES

THE NATIONAL ACADEMIES PRESS
Washington, DC
www.nap.edu

THE NATIONAL ACADEMIES PRESS
500 Fifth Street, NW • Washington, DC 20001

NOTICE: The project that is the subject of this report was approved by the Governing Board of the National Research Council, whose members are drawn from the councils of the National Academy of Sciences, the National Academy of Engineering, and the Institute of Medicine. The members of the committee responsible for the report were chosen for their special competences and with regard for appropriate balance.

This project was sponsored by the Defense Advanced Research Projects Agency under award number MDA972-02-1-0005. The content of this report does not necessarily reflect the position or the policy of the government, and no official endorsement should be inferred. Any opinions, findings, conclusions, or recommendations expressed in this report are those of the members of the committee and do not necessarily reflect the views of the sponsors.

International Standard Book Number 0-309-08530-6

Additional copies of this report are available from

The National Academies Press
500 Fifth Street, NW
Box 285
Washington, DC 20055
800/624-6242
202/334-3313 (in the Washington Metropolitan Area)
<http://www.nap.edu>

Suggested citation: National Research Council (2002) *Discouraging Terrorism: Some Implications of 9/11*. Panel on Understanding Terrorists in Order to Deter Terrorism. Neil J. Smelser and Faith Mitchell, editors. Division of Behavioral and Social Sciences and Education. Washington, DC: The National Academies Press.

THE NATIONAL ACADEMIES
Advisers to the Nation on Science, Engineering, and Medicine

The **National Academy of Sciences** is a private, nonprofit, self-perpetuating society of distinguished scholars engaged in scientific and engineering research, dedicated to the furtherance of science and technology and to their use for the general welfare. Upon the authority of the charter granted to it by the Congress in 1863, the Academy has a mandate that requires it to advise the federal government on scientific and technical matters. Dr. Bruce M. Alberts is president of the National Academy of Sciences.

The **National Academy of Engineering** was established in 1964, under the charter of the National Academy of Sciences, as a parallel organization of outstanding engineers. It is autonomous in its administration and in the selection of its members, sharing with the National Academy of Sciences the responsibility for advising the federal government. The National Academy of Engineering also sponsors engineering programs aimed at meeting national needs, encourages education and research, and recognizes the superior achievements of engineers. Dr. Wm. A. Wulf is president of the National Academy of Engineering.

The **Institute of Medicine** was established in 1970 by the National Academy of Sciences to secure the services of eminent members of appropriate professions in the examination of policy matters pertaining to the health of the public. The Institute acts under the responsibility given to the National Academy of Sciences by its congressional charter to be an adviser to the federal government and, upon its own initiative, to identify issues of medical care, research, and education. Dr. Harvey V. Fineberg is president of the Institute of Medicine.

The **National Research Council** was organized by the National Academy of Sciences in 1916 to associate the broad community of science and technology with the Academy's purposes of furthering knowledge and advising the federal government. Functioning in accordance with general policies determined by the Academy, the Council has become the principal operating agency of both the National Academy of Sciences and the National Academy of Engineering in providing services to the government, the public, and the scientific and engineering communities. The Council is administered jointly by both Academies and the Institute of Medicine. Dr. Bruce M. Alberts and Dr. Wm. A. Wulf are chair and vice chair, respectively, of the National Research Council.

www.national-academies.org

PANEL ON UNDERSTANDING TERRORISTS IN ORDER TO DETER TERRORISM 2002

NEIL J. SMELSER (*Chair*), Department of Sociology (emeritus), University of California, Berkeley

ROBERT McCORMICK ADAMS, Department of Anthropology, University of California, San Diego

LISA ANDERSON, School of International and Public Affairs, Columbia University

NAZLI CHOUCRI, Department of Political Science and the Technology and Development Program, Massachusetts Institute of Technology

MARTHA CRENSHAW, Department of Government, Wesleyan University

EUGENE A. HAMMEL, Departments of Anthropology and Demography (emeritus), University of California, Berkeley

ARIE W. KRUGLANSKI, Department of Psychology, University of Maryland

TIMOTHY McDANIEL, Department of Sociology, University of California, San Diego

PHYLLIS OAKLEY, Career Foreign Service Officer (retired), U.S. Department of State

THOMAS C. SCHELLING, School of Public Affairs, University of Maryland

JOHN VOLL, Edward A. Walsh School of Foreign Service, Georgetown University

FAITH MITCHELL, *Study Director*

JANET GARTON, *Program Associate*

BENJAMIN WOOLSEY, *Project Assistant*

Contents

---

*The appendix is not printed in this volume but is available online. Go to http://www.nap.edu and search for *Discouraging Terrorism: Some Implications of 9/11.*

Preface

The national scientific community is as aware of and concerned with the contemporary terrorist threat to the nation as all other segments of American society. Consistent with this posture, the presidents of the National Academies—the National Academy of Sciences, the Institute of Medicine, and the National Academy of Engineering—wrote a letter on September 20, 2001, to President George W. Bush pledging the scientific resources of the nation, as represented in the National Academies, to help contend with the new national crisis.

Also consistent with the relevance of scientific knowledge for understanding and contending with terrorism, in October 2001 the Defense Advanced Research Projects Agency (DARPA) of the U.S. Department of Defense approached the Division of Behavioral and Social Sciences and Education of the National Research Council (NRC) to conduct a study of "what terrorists value." That phrase conveyed a request to identify the ingredients of terrorists' mentality and situation that are positively meaningful to them and that might be deterred by threat or inducement. The NRC formed the panel, and the material in these pages constitutes our report. The panel's activities ran parallel to but had different emphases from the National Academies' own Committee on Science and Technology for Countering Terrorism, which concentrated on the role of science and technology in defending the nation against terrorist attacks. That committee's report is entitled *Making the Nation Safer: The Role of Science and Technology in Countering Terrorism* (National Research Council, 2002).

From the beginning, the panel realized how difficult the DARPA charge was, given the complex and only partially understood situation of international terrorism and terrorists. Accordingly, we determined to take a multilevel approach to the charge and address it from all angles that seemed potentially fruitful. Beginning with the most immediate and direct approach—deterrence—we evaluate that strategy and suggest both limitations and appropriate adaptations of it in dealing with terrorism. We call special attention to the role of third parties in the deterrence of terrorists. The panel also identifies the kinds of audiences that are important to terrorists as well as their special network mode of organization, focusing on both the assets and vulnerabilities of each. We also specify certain long-term international, demographic, economic, political, and cultural conditions that are conducive to terrorist activity and its support. Effective modification of these conditions might diminish the impulses favoring terrorism.

The panel includes scholars of anthropology, demography, economics, history, political science, psychology, and sociology. Their special areas of expertise include the study of terrorism itself, the contemporary Middle East, Islamic history and religion, revolutionary social movements, deterrence and game theory, the cognitive structure of beliefs, and the politics of diplomacy and peacekeeping. The panel had a preliminary discussion on January 14 and held formal meetings on February 25 and April 5, 2002. Between meetings we coordinated the drafting and review of materials. The face-to-face meetings were especially valuable in synthesizing knowledge about terrorism in general and keeping focused on the special charge given to us. We read widely in diverse strands of literature but did not consult any classified material.

The panel was responsible for completing this report in a record four-month period. We would like to thank the National Research Council staff who supported our work and facilitated the achievement of this ambitious goal: Faith Mitchell, study director, Janet Garton, research assistant, and Benjamin Woolsey, project assistant. Erik Smith worked as a consultant with Eugene Hammel on groundbreaking demographic analysis. The panel is grateful as well to DARPA for its financial support.

This report has been reviewed in draft form by individuals chosen for their diverse perspectives and technical expertise, in accordance with procedures approved by the Report Review Committee of the NRC. The purpose of this independent review is to provide candid and critical comments that will assist the institution in making its published report as sound as possible and to ensure that the report meets institutional standards for objectivity, evidence, and responsiveness to the study charge. The review comments and draft manuscript remain confidential to protect the integrity of the deliberative process.

We thank the following individuals for their participation in the review of this report: Coleen Conway-Welch, School of Nursing, Vanderbilt University; Martin E. Marty, Fairfax M. Cone Distinguished Service Professor, University of Chicago; Clark McCauley, Psychology Department, Bryn Mawr College; Daniel S. Nagin, H. J. Heinz School of Public Policy, Carnegie Mellon University; Melford E. Spiro, Department of Anthropology, University of California, San Diego; and Edward Wenk, Professor Emeritus of Engineering, Public Affairs, and Social Management of Technology, University of Washington.

Although the reviewers listed above have provided many constructive comments and suggestions, they were not asked to endorse the conclusions or recommendations nor did they see the final draft of the report before its release. The review of this report was overseen by Robert Frosch, Belfer Center for Science and International Affairs, Harvard University, and Charles Tilly, Departments of Sociology and Political Science, Columbia University. Appointed by the National Research Council, they were responsible for making certain that an independent examination of this report was carried out in accordance with institutional procedures and that all review comments were carefully considered. Responsibility for the final content of this report rests entirely with the authoring panel and the institution. Finally, the panel also thanks Michael Teitelbaum, Sloan Foundation, who reviewed the paper by Hammel and Smith that appears as the Appendix (on line only).

> Neil J. Smelser, *Chair*
> Panel on Understanding Terrorists in
> Order to Deter Terrorism

Executive Summary

This report addresses the question of what terrorists hold in value, a question asked in order to assess some means and strategies for deterring, deflecting, or preventing terrorist activities. We approach the question at several levels, moving from the use of short-term deterrent strategies to the modification of the broader contexts and conditions conducive to terrorist activities in the long run. We focus on contemporary Islamic terrorism but deal with generic dimensions in many instances.

The report does not address domestic, or homeland, aspects of terrorism, which are covered in detail in two National Academies reports, *Making the Nation Safer: The Role of Science and Technology in Countering Terrorism* (National Research Council, 2002) and *Terrorism: Perspectives from the Behavioral and Social Sciences* (National Research Council, in press). Nor does it recommend policy strategies based on the application of its conclusions.

Deterrence as a known strategy is demonstrated to have a positive role in contending with terrorists, though terrorism poses special problems that limit its effectiveness and call for modifications. Among those problems are (a) difficulties in getting unambiguous and credible threats across to terrorists, (b) the unwillingness of terrorists to communicate except indirectly and on their own terms, (c) exceptionally high levels of mutual distrust, (d) uncertainty about how to affect what terrorists value, and (e) uncertainty about the targets to which threats should be directed.

In light of these problems, the best policy may be one of deterrent threats combined with policies of working with and through third parties who may have the capacity to influence terrorists. Among such parties are state regimes that harbor terrorists, moderate political and social groups in such states, neighboring regimes, and U.S. allies.

Terrorists carry out their activities before a number of different audiences— potential recruits, their own memberships, states and politically interested groupings ("sentiment pools") in societies in which they operate, the media and its imagined readership, audiences in enemy societies, and the audience of "world public opinion." These audiences are both sources of potential support and foci of vulnerability for terrorism.

Terrorist organizations are typically far-flung networks that rely on secrecy, invisibility, flexibility, extreme commitment on the part of members, and coordination of military-like activities as their trademarks. These features are sources of both strength and vulnerability.

Moving to broader contexts and conditions, we identify three factors that help explain the rise of terrorism as a form of activity: the great asymmetry of economic, political, and military power in the world; the availability of weapons of mass destruction; and the permeability of world society occasioned by processes of globalization.

With respect to political context, terrorism and its supporting audiences appear to be fostered by policies of extreme political repression and discouraged by policies of incorporating both dissident and moderate groups responsibly into civil society and the political process.

With respect to economic and social conditions, many societies that foster terrorism are characterized by high population growth and large numbers of disadvantaged youth and by extreme economic inequality and poverty. When these conditions combine with strong—sometimes religiously reinforced—anti-Western ideologies, a fertile field for supporting terrorism is generated.

RECOMMENDATIONS

The panel ventures the several specific recommendations about deterrence and prevention that follow from our analysis:

- Deterrence, understood conventionally as the direct use

of threats, punishments, and inducements to prevent enemy action, has a viable place in dealing with terrorists (supporting text, pp. 8-14).

- Many of the assumptions of conventional deterrence, however—availability of channels of communication, credibility among communicating parties, knowing what adversaries value—are not likely to be present in contemporary terrorist situations. As a result, reliance on direct deterrence can be only somewhat effective. In addition, direct threats and perceived overretaliation may have counterproductive effects with respect to generating support for terrorist groups and activities by previously uncommitted audiences (supporting text, pp. 10-14).

- Direct efforts to deter should therefore be accompanied by working through all available third parties—societies hosting terrorist organizations, countries trusted by host societies, or the United States's own allies—who may have more credibility with and influence on terrorist organizations than this country, as enemy, does (supporting text, pp. 14-16).

- Whenever possible, policies should be directed toward distancing and alienating relevant audiences from terrorist organizations and activities. The incorporation of potentially extremist political groups into the civil society of actual and potential host societies is especially important (supporting text, pp. 16-22).

- Intelligence, infiltration, and related activities should be directed at points of vulnerability of terrorist organizations—their reliance on audience, their ideological inflexibility, their problems of maintaining commitments, and their potential for organizational failure (supporting text, pp. 22-25).

- The social conditions fostering the use of terrorism are complex and include demographic, economic, political, and educational factors. In the long run, preventive strategies should include improving these conditions in countries vulnerable to terrorist organizations and activities, as a means of diminishing the probabilities of their emergence and crystallization (supporting text, pp. 25-31).

The one sure conclusion emerging from this report about strategies for countering terrorism is that there are no silver bullets or quick fixes available. It is possible to specify more effective and less effective deterrent and preventive policies at various levels and under different conditions. However, the general policy approach has to be adaptive, opportunistic, and multisided. The conventional problem-solving logic so attractive in American culture—find a problem and then fix it—is of limited utility, and a longer term, more contextualized approach is necessary.

Discouraging Terrorism: Some Implications of 9/11

The panel was given both an abbreviated charge and an elaborated one. The first was to bring behavioral and social science knowledge to bear on the question, "What do terrorists value?" with an eye to influencing their behavior by affecting what they value.

In considering, studying, and reflecting on this brief charge, the committee ultimately concluded that to provide simple, direct, and unambiguous answers to the question is not possible. In addressing the abbreviated version of the charge, the panel faced the following formidable obstacles:

- Terrorists committed to secrecy have little interest in communicating what they value from motivational and strategic points of view.
- Some inferences about what terrorists value can be drawn from what targets they attack, why they say they are attacking them, and statements about their own beliefs, but such inferences are necessarily indirect and often speculative.
- It is reasonable to assume that what terrorists value is not at all static but changes according to (a) their changing sense of the opportunities that are open or possible for them, (b) the changing outlooks of their leaders, (c) the outlooks of those whom they hope will support them, and (d) the postures and the expected and actual responses of those they attack.

In considering these obstacles, the panel decided that it would not be responsible to spin out a list of what terrorists value and a corresponding list of threats to destroy or take away what they value.

Accordingly, the panel devised a strategy that we regard as taking seriously the abbreviated charge but also taking into account the complexities of contemporary terrorism. In this effort we were guided in part by the expanded charge, which contained both a general and a specific request. The first request was to "examine the social, cultural, organizational, and psychological context of the terrorism now directed at the U.S., and the implications for new approaches to deter terrorism." The second was to pay attention to "what terrorists value, as a means of developing effective strategies for deterring terrorist acts." The first assignment calls for a social science analysis of conditions and contexts—and how they might be affected in the interests of dealing with terrorism. The second implies a more immediate, strategic line of thinking.

These two assignments blend into one another. On one hand, what terrorists value is found in large part in the context of their cultural beliefs, in the ways they organize themselves, and in their motivational and group psychology. On the other, according to the logic of deterrence, the appropriate strategies are to threaten to take away, impair, or destroy what they value— or, alternatively, to offer inducements that are meaningful in terms of what they value—so that they will be prevented from launching attacks on the United States. A more enduring result is to affect the lives and situations of terrorists so that they will not *want* to attack the country.

This very blending made our task formidable, because contemporary terrorism and what terrorists value are bred by multiple causes and, correspondingly, no single preventive solution can be realistically envisioned. Furthermore, the historically novel combination of elements in current terrorist activities— their clandestine networks of organization, their capacity to use new technologies, and the particular ideologies they live by— call for a reexamination of warlike conflict and ways of dealing with it.

We have approached our assignment at several different levels of analysis in order to unscramble these complexities and to identify more precisely the points at which sanctions and policies might be relevant. The report discusses both discouraging terrorism, which in the long term depends on support and recruits from the sympathy pool, and discouraging current terrorists. We begin with the immediate and situational aspects of terrorism as it now threatens the nation, posing the question of short-term deterrence. Deterrence theory as it has evolved is a useful way of thinking, but it must be tailored to the current circumstances. Next we look at the audiences of terrorists, which operate—but only crudely and approximately—as a kind of public opinion in their environment and which they care about and value. Then we consider the nature and vulnerabilities of the specific organizational forms of contemporary terrorism, and in what sense these might be targets for making terrorist activities fail. Then, moving toward even more remote and general causes, we consider the political, demographic, and economic contexts of terrorism. At this stage we consider conditions and determinants of contemporary terrorism—what facilitates and discourages its development as a form of conflict—and move into the arena of long-term policy issues. We do not recommend specific economic, political, and foreign policies, or reactions to the attacks of September 11—that lies beyond the compass of our charge—but we give our best account of the considerations that might serve as background for such policies.

The scope of the report precluded the panel's exploration of several important, related topics. These include the evolution of individuals and groups into terrorism, the opportunities for deterrence presented by specific cultural and religious values, the variety of paths to conflict and warfare, and the particular circumstances of the September 11 attacks.

A lengthy review of the literature is also beyond the scope of this report. Several useful sources are referenced in the text that follows. Additional scholarly and informative analyses include Wieviorka (1993); Pillar (2001); Hoffman (1998); Schmid et al., (1988); Lewis (2002); and Stout (in press).

Finally, in responding to our assignments, we focus largely on Islamic terrorists and the problem of deterring them. We also focus on terrorism directed toward American targets in this country and abroad. There are practical and political reasons for this narrowing of the topic, because Islamic terrorism is, at the moment, the most salient threat to the nation—the elephant in the living room, as it were. In addition, the resources available to the panel and the short time-line for our work prevented us from covering the entire range of what is called terrorism. At the same time, we recognize the analytic limitations of this narrowing.

For example, we exclude from consideration many varieties of terrorism—separatist and independence movements, suicide bombers in Israel, domestic terrorism by antiabortion and antipollution activists and others. Were we to extend the analysis historically to include everything we understand to be terrorism, we would work from a generic definition, such as the illegal use or threatened use of force or violence with the intent to coerce, treating Islamic terrorism as a special case, and focusing on its anti-Western and religious dimensions. If we were to consider terrorism in general, we would also have to extend and qualify many statements in this report. Despite the narrowed focus, however, some of our observations do apply in varying degree to terrorism in general.

We also exclude discussion of the domestic reactions to terrorism. For this, the reader is referred to the reports, *Making the Nation Safer: The Role of Science and Technology in Countering Terrorism* (National Research Council, 2002) and *Terrorism: Perspectives from the Behavioral and Social Sciences* (National Research Council, in press), which present a consideration of some of the general aspects of terrorism, including implications for homeland security.

· ·

TERRORISTS' MOTIVES, VALUES, AND ORGANIZATION

DETERRENCE AND TERRORISM

Deterrence as an ingredient of conflict is age-old. Theoretical understanding as well as refined applications of it are more recent, a product of the cold war period of conflict between the United States and its allies and the Soviet bloc and international communism in general (Schelling, 1966; Pape, 1996). The idea of deterrence has also been developed in the study of such topics as crime prevention, drug dealing, and the behavior of employees (Nagin, 1998, Kleiman, 1992, Schelling, 1984). As a result of its apparently successful exercise in the era of superpower confrontation, deterrence comes readily to mind as an effective defense against terrorism—to deter terrorists by coercive threats and inducements. However, contemporary terrorism looks very different from many other warlike situations and, as a result, creates limitations on deterrence as we have come to understand it and calls for adaptations in our thinking.

Deterrence comes from the Latin root that means "to frighten." Its simple definition is to prevent or discourage a party from acting by creating fear or doubt. Deterring is a form of coercing others not to act, but coercion may also involve compelling them actively to comply or act in a way they would not otherwise have done—the term "compellence" has been coined to describe this. Iraq illustrates the difference between deterrence and compellence. The United States hopes to deter the regime of Saddam Hussein from acquiring or using weapons of mass destruction (or from attacking Kuwait or Israel or other neighbors), but it may also need to compel the regime to disclose, to let inspectors in, to disarm, or to resign.

Deterrence is essentially passive, focused on preserving the status quo. It requires no action as long as the adversary does nothing; it requires action by the deterrer only when the status quo is violated. Compellence usually requires a deadline or some coercive action until the adversary complies. Giving in to deterrence can also have a face-saving aspect; neither the Soviet Union nor the North Atlantic Treaty Organization (NATO) ever had to say that they had hostile intentions that they were afraid to carry out, even though this appeared to be the case. Complying with compelling demands is more public because it calls for more active, conspicuous behavior on the part of the adversary being compelled. Being deterred has no aftermath; it simply means that an adversary does not act over an indefinite period. Compelling demands can be said to have been met if the adversary complies. Furthermore, unlike deterrence, giving in to compellence is in principle identifiable—though often difficult to ensure, even with surveillance—and it often sets off a new set of demands, that is, some kind of compensation for complying.

Interestingly, terrorism and deterrence shade into one another, because both rely on creating fear in an adversary. Terrorism, particularly when it has political goals on its agenda, involves committing acts of violence (that presumably induce terror) to gain its ends, however tenuous and remote the hope that the attacked nation will comply with its demands. In that sense, political terrorism is a diffuse form of compelling behavior. Deterrence usually involves threats to use violence as an ultimate action, but that violence is reserved for retaliation when an adversary steps over a line that has been defined as a limit.

In the literature on deterrence a distinction is made between deterrence proper, that is, capitalizing on fear generated by threat, and "deterrence by denial," or opposing attacks so effectively that the adversary cannot achieve its objective. The principle of denial lies behind the efforts to control the borders of the society and to harden or make inaccessible anticipated targets of terrorist attack. In this report we push the logic of prevention even further and consider, as a part of long-term prevention, the broad conditions of terrorism. Modifying those conditions may be said to be an indirect and long-term way of deterring terrorism, though it does so by softening its impulse rather than creating fear or doubt.

To return to deterrence in its simpler form, we note several conditions that must be met for it to be successful: first, a threat has to come across unambiguously to the adversary; second, the threat if carried out has to be painful and costly to the adversary; and third, it has to be credible, that is, it must induce in the adversary the belief that the deterrer can, or probably can, fulfill the threat. The last condition, ironically, presupposes a weak variation of trust—not the sort bred by solidarity or mutual affection, but a belief that the other will behave in accord with the stated intentions.

The problem bedeviling efforts to rely on deterrence in dealing with contemporary terrorism is that every one of these conditions is met only imperfectly if at all. In this connection we make the following observations:

- Successful deterrence is often mutual. The Soviets were probably deterred from attacking westward during the cold war, and NATO was deterred from making a preemptive movement into Warsaw Pact territories. The hope is that India and Pakistan may be moving toward a similar mutuality in which clear definitions of lines not to be crossed by either side come to be well articulated and understood. In contrast, the contemporary terrorist situation involves an asymmetry rather than a mutuality. On their side, the United States and its allies are clearly interested in deterring terrorist actions of all sorts. Yet deterrence is not a precise or helpful notion in characterizing the current orientations and goals of terrorists. It is difficult to imagine that terrorists rely on threats of attacks or actual attacks to *deter* the United States and its allies from retaliating (the threat of nuclear attacks is an evident exception). In fact, such attacks come closer to inviting retaliation, given the enormous power differential between international terrorist organizations and the nations they attack. Furthermore, retaliation by the United States may be in fact "welcomed" as a way to "prove" victimization of the terrorists and a means to mobilize the uncommitted, particularly if there is collateral damage of civilian targets. Neither does the idea of "lines not to be crossed" seem to apply. While terrorists operate within certain kinds of constraint on their actions, a condition of their success is to strike with surprise on often unanticipated targets, to rule no target out altogether, and to capitalize on ambiguity and uncertainty rather than defined understandings. In a word, deterrence is not much in the vocabulary of terrorists. Depending on its type of ideological framing, terrorist activities tend to be defined as attacking a general source of evil in the world, as defined by an anti-American or anti-Western mentality; as a means to gain certain political ends (withdrawal of troops, end of support for Israel); or as actions consistent with a fundamentalist religious mission.

  • The conditions for being able to communicate with terrorists are not easily realized. There are known cases in which actual or threatened terror is used instrumentally as an entrée for negotiation. However, in many cases, the premium on the terrorist side is on secrecy and *not* communicating directly with or being communicated to by the enemy. Because terrorism thrives on secrecy and surprise, enemy knowledge of terrorists' whereabouts and possible intentions—likely to be revealed by direct communication—places them at a disadvantage. Most of the "communicating" done by many terrorist organizations is either by attacking without notice, by sometimes (but not always) taking credit for attacks through various media, or by otherwise communicating indirectly through their favored audiences. The idea of being communicated with by adversaries is often ruled out because it compromises the whole foundation of secrecy and undermines the purpose of terrorism.

  • The level of mutual suspicion and distrust among adversaries in the contemporary terrorist situation is so high that credibility is weak and sometimes nonexistent. In some cases, threats, if believed, can be effective even though adversaries distrust one another; the cold war produced many instances of this. The key element is not precisely trust but credibility; even if adversaries regard one another as mortal enemies, deterrence can be effective if they believe their enemies' threats and believe that they will be acted on. In other cases, extreme distrust makes for distortions of communication and, consequently, dilution of credibility.

The ideologies involved also matter. If, as is often the case, the terrorist ideology is that the West is committed to dominating or destroying Islamic societies and religion (Shuja, 2001; Pollack, 2001), then *any* communication can be turned into an untrustworthy one. Consider, for example, the airing of the explanation in some Muslim countries that the attacks on the World Trade Center and the Pentagon on September 11, 2001, were a Jewish plot designed to mobilize the might of the West to attack the Arab countries; consider also the widespread accusation that the videotape showing Osama bin Laden boasting about the destruction on September 11 was a Western fabrication.

More generally, if the terrorist ideology calls for an undaunted and absolute war—as some versions of fundamentalist Islam ideologies do—then adherents may hold the belief that they are undeterrable or that efforts to deter do not matter to them. Distrust also runs high on the American side, and to the degree that citizens reciprocate the terrorists' worldview by believing terrorism to be an unqualified evil, this mentality augments their suspicion and perhaps diminishes their effectiveness. To venture these insights is not to assign blame but to diagnose. And the diagnosis is that under conditions of extreme mutual suspicion, the probabilities for successful deterrence are weakened.

• Successful deterrence depends on a reasonably accurate knowledge of what the enemy values, that is, what the enemy is not willing to lose. In the case of the Soviet Union it was clear that it valued its national life and existence as framed by the Communist ideology of the time and, in the end, was not willing to risk its obliteration. The Western countries valued the same (though framed in an ideology of freedom and Western capitalism) and were willing to settle for a policy of containment rather than aggression.

What terrorists value is more difficult to determine. Certainly they value their own lives, except under the condition of the decision, made on their own terms, that suicide is justified by the overriding importance of personal salvation or group cause. They value their families, their organizations, their comrades, their weapons, their financial support, their way of life, and their vision of the future. The importance of this vision of the future is well articulated by Hoffman (1998, p.169), "All terrorists, however, doubtless have one trait in common: they live in the future: that distant—yet imperceptibly close—point in time when they will assuredly triumph over their enemies and attain the ultimate realization of their political destiny. For the religious groups, this future is divinely decreed and the terrorists themselves specifically anointed to achieve it. The inevitability of their victory is taken for granted." They value their own cultural values and, if these are religiously based, their religious commitments. If religious commitment is part of the picture, they are likely to regard themselves as moral actors, doing violence to others and even to themselves for good and sufficient reasons. In the case of committed Muslim terrorists, strong elements of honor, shame, and revenge are often salient.

Sometimes what they value can be affected (for example, attempting to close off sources of financial support through the international banking system). In many cases, however, direct threats to take away or destroy what terrorists value are not viable because they are not believed or because they cannot be readily carried out. Terrorists may know that their enemy can destroy them in the long run, but if they believe it cannot retaliate in the short run, they may proceed anyway. Finally, terrorist organizations, though their operations are often located in part within states, are usually stateless in that they do not have the responsibility of governing and defending national integrity and cannot be directly or readily influenced by threats to nations.

From these observations we conclude that direct deterrence by clearly communicating credible warnings and threats to terrorists is of limited utility in comparison to other types of wartime situations. There are several ways in which deterrent threats can fail. First, the threat never gets made, because it is not known (by the party likely to be attacked) what the assault might be (though the World Trade Center was known to be a potential target mainly because of its 1993 bombing, it was not feasible to issue a specific threat that if it was bombed, then specific enemies could expect specific consequences). Second, the adversary may not believe a threat if made; as indicated, terrorists have a combination of motives and ideological values conducive to such disbelief. For example, what is intended as a threat may be received as a provocation. Third, even if the threat is heard and understood, it may fail because terrorists may decide that the gain from challenging it is worth the antici-pated cost—again, a plausible response, given their worldview. Fourth, given the far-flung nature of terrorist networks, it may not be clear who are the "they" one wishes to deter. It is likely that terrorists are not a single actor who is reachable by threats but rather a diverse coalition of people who may not be in full command of their own forces. And finally, deterrence, even if it "works," is limited in that it does not work to remove the political and social determinants of terrorism and is therefore not a substitute for policies that might do so.

All this is not to conclude that deterrence cannot be a viable strategy in the current circumstances. Perhaps if the Taliban regime in Afghanistan had believed that it would cease to exist (which it has for all practical purposes) in the event of a terrorist attack on the United States, it may have acted to discourage such an attack on the part of the Al Qaeda organization. If Al Qaeda had anticipated and believed that its organization would be possibly fatally damaged and in any event crippled and dispersed, it may have bided its time and made other calcula-tions. The facts that the Taliban lost control of Afghanistan and Al Qaeda was wounded no doubt constitute a credible warning to other states harboring terrorists—and perhaps terrorists them-selves—that the United States is willing to act and that it has a destructive capacity to destroy what terrorists value by killing them or otherwise rendering them ineffective.

This line of reasoning suggests the importance of relying on the help of third parties in efforts to deter. If terrorists are determined not to communicate with adversaries except in their chosen ways, if they cannot be communicated with directly, if they do not understand or believe what is communicated by their principal and deeply distrusted adversaries, then logic dictates that one should, as an element of overall strategy, rely in part on *others* who might be able to communicate with them more effectively and with greater credibility. Several implica-tions flow from this general point.

• State-to-state relations should be maintained with states friendly to terrorist activity or those who have harbored terror-ists. Because of the depth of the terrorist threat, it is tempting for the United States to assume mainly a threatening or punitive posture toward those states. Certainly those states should be the object of deterrent threats. But at the same time, they can also serve to help make the threats credible to terrorist organizations in their midst, because these states have greater credibility in their communications with them than their adversaries do. To be sure, this strategy is an uncertain one with many possibilities of slippage, both because such states usually have limited affection and trust for the United States and because they also have fragile relations with—and cannot control completely—the terrorist organizations in their midst. The logic underlying this argument is that communication with terrorists is extraordinarily difficult, and any means possible should be kept open.

- Some work may be accomplished by working with moderate agencies *within* such societies that do not condone terrorism but that exist side by side in the political and social system with terrorist organizations and may be sources of influence on them. We have in mind two kinds of agencies in these countries: (a) moderate political parties that may or may not be friendly to the West but that have chosen to work by means of exerting political influence within the rules of the political game and (b) educational institutions at all levels—scientific academies, universities, colleges, secondary and primary systems—that stand side by side with but serve as important counterbalances to the radical Islamic schools that teach and instill virulent anti-Western views.

- Relations should also be maintained with nations that have had a history of friendliness toward anti-Western terrorism but whose political postures have turned around to some degree (for example, Libya, Egypt, and Pakistan share such a history, though there are differences among them). If relations with the United States are solid enough, these states can be used as intermediaries to communicate with other nations in their region with less friendly relations to the United States but who trust their neighbors more and are more likely to give credibility to them. Similar types of intermediary roles might be envisioned for the United Nations (UN) and for nations that are generally perceived as neutral or have participated in peacekeeping activities.

- Another set of third parties is U.S. allies—mainly Western—who share vulnerability to terrorism and also share the U.S. attitude of enmity toward terrorism. Three points should be noted: (a) Deterrence by coalition is hard to manage, as evidenced by the failure of allies to agree on objectives and force commitments in the Congo in the 1960s and Bosnia in the 1990s (Winner, 2002). The pattern more likely to be effective is U.S. leadership while securing cooperation and support from friends. (b) In the main, U.S. allies are not as likely to be as aggressive or steadfast in their commitments against terrorism. This is understandable given the lesser vulnerability of many of those countries, even though Great Britain, France, and other countries are likely targets of international terrorism. (c) To ask allies to support U.S. antiterrorist activity also means asking them to assume the cost of exposure to attacks, and this has to be acknowledged. These three points pose special challenges for the United States, which has much to lose by going it alone and must continuously persuade others to be relentless and to stay on board while also listening to them responsibly.

The conclusion to be drawn from these arguments is that the contemporary terrorist situation, as it has evolved, enforces a certain *indirectness* in the use of deterrent measures that involve threats meant to supplement—but stopping short of—a brute force policy of rooting out and destroying terrorists at any opportunity. As indicated, direct threats still have a place, but they are not likely to be effective on their own. Because of the special difficulties involved, the nation needs all the friends it can secure in efforts to deter terrorism.

AUDIENCES FOR TERRORISTS: SIX SUBSETS

AUDIENCES FOR TERRORISTS

— Potential Recruits
— Internal Audience
— Host Societies
— Media
— Enemy Societies
— World Opinion

While terrorist organizations are secretive and not accountable, they nevertheless regard their status with various audiences as important for their survival, effectiveness, and success. Very little is known about the dynamics of terrorist-audience relations, but audiences are so important to them—and constitute potential sources of vulnerability—that some words about them need to be said.

The issue of audiences arises in six different ways, as outlined below and described in the sections that follow.

Potential Recruits

The first audience is that of potential recruits. Recruits to terrorist organizations do not come from a single class of individuals (e.g., alienated middle class, down-and-outers) (McCauley, in press, Library of Congress, 1999; Maddy-Weitzman, 1996; Krueger and Maleckova, 2002; Hamzeh, 1997; Sivan, 1997; Abootalebi, 1999; Alam, 2000). Furthermore, the paths and processes by which any given individual becomes a terrorist are idiosyncratic, both in terms of when and how he or she becomes alienated from some important aspect of life and in terms of when that alienation transforms itself into participation in terrorist activities (Kellen, 1979; Library of Congress, 1999; Sprinzak, 1998). The precise supply of terrorists is unknown, and while recruiters know of some fruitful sources—for example, those who have attended schools and mosques that preach virulent anti-Americanism and militant and fundamentalist Islam—the actual process of recruitment is highly uncertain, as it is for any extremist social movement (Lofland, 1966; Erickson, 1981).

One important way of affecting the potential supply of recruits is to strive to incorporate the groups from which they derive into the general political processes of the countries in which they reside—into parties, pressure groups, or coalitions of voters (Ferracuti, 1998). Meaningful involvement in civil society makes the groups involved responsible and thereby operates as a deflection if not direct deterrent of extremist activities. Meaningful involvement in the more informal side of civil society—family, friends, and occupation—may also provide a certain inhibition to recruitment for extremist activity (Hoffman, 2001).

Internal Audience

The internal audience is in terrorist organizations themselves. One of the most important features of gaining and holding recruits is the group dynamics involved (McCauley, in press, 2002). After recruitment, a definite process unfolds: isolating the individual from outside conflicts, indoctrination, cultivating loyalty to comrades, and giving instructions and training about future activities (see Bandura, 1998). The primary group of dedicated comrades comes to overshadow but at the same time reinforces other kinds of commitment. Whatever the original reasons for joining, the individual becomes entrapped. At the same time—at least, according to interviews with some terrorists—the process generates anxiety for having crossed a point of no return, problems of dealing with flagging of enthusiasm and commitment during long periods of inactivity (or outright renunciation of the terrorist activities by a political organization), and a level of coerciveness and mistrust among comrades, bred from the suspicion and dread of potential defectors (Kellen, 1979). Because of these internal pressures, forced inactivity can actually cause a terrorist group to come apart. For organizations that include terrorists but also have members who carry out teaching and other social activities, the latter constitute another kind of internal audience whose attention and loyalty are important.

Host Societies

Terrorist organizations maintain a variety of relationships with the nations in which they conduct their activities. Some countries sympathetic to terrorists play host to them by not repressing them, permitting training camps, and so on. And some states themselves have sponsored terrorism or engaged in it. Especially in cases in which terrorist organizations are given support or encouragement, the host society becomes a relevant audience for terrorists. It is important to cultivate relations with them, to curry support from relevant groups and politicians in those societies. Miscalculations and mistakes can cost the support of host states; this, of course, is a source of vulnerability for a terrorist group, which must then dedicate more of its energies to its "foreign relations" with states, resisting repression on the part of those states by going underground or leaving the country altogether. In all events, the host state is a relevant audience.

In addition, the societies from which terrorist groups arise or operate are made up of a diversity of social groups (intellectuals, religious believers, political interests) who constitute potential "sentiment pools" that are sources of support or lack of support for extremist groups and terrorist activities (see Snow et al., 1986). These groups are not themselves involved in terrorism, but their orientations toward it are important. They may be turned off by what they regard as terrorist excesses; they may be drawn to support terrorists if they come to regard them as persecuted martyrs. This kind of public opinion is an important determinant of the fate of the terrorist impulse in societies in which it is present. Needless to say, involvement of these groups in the processes of civil society also tends to have a moderating influence on the opinions of their members.

Media

The media that report terrorist activities—as well as the imagined readership of those media—are another very powerful and gratifying audience. The media constitute an important avenue for the attention-getting potential of terrorist activities, which constitutes one element in the psychological makeup of terrorists (Post, 1998). The coverage of terrorists in the media and public awareness about them has been noticeable for some time, but they skyrocketed to a high and sustained level after September 11.

There is no large and significant public event—the Olympics, an economic summit, an important gathering of officials—that is not accompanied by worry about security and the threat of terrorist activity. The amount of literature devoted to terrorism is of unprecedented proportions. Osama bin Laden was considered as a contender for *Time* magazine's "Man of the Year" for 2002, an award that ultimately went to New York Mayor Rudolph Giuliani. The issue that drew attention to both was terrorism.

Sprinzak (2001) has gone so far as to suggest a new brand of terrorism that he calls "the megalomaniac hyperterrorist," by which he means self-anointed individuals with larger-than-life callings: Ramzi Youssef (the man behind the 1993 World Trade Center bombing), Shoko Asahara (leader of Aum Shinrikyo and architect of the 1995 gas attack in a Tokyo subway station), Timothy McVeigh (the 1995 Oklahoma City bomber), Igal Amir (who assassinated Itzhak Rabin), and Osama bin Laden all had in common the urge to use catastrophic attacks in order to write a new chapter in history. This characterization should be taken as a simple psychological explanation of some terrorist activities, but Sprinzak has highlighted the intrinsic concern with audience as a key ingredient in the terrorist mentality.

Enemy Societies

Another audience is that of enemy societies. The vast majority of terrorist attacks have a political objective. Sometimes these are highly specific, as in the case of the favored forms of terrorism in the 1970s, hijacking and kidnapping, which were typically accompanied by a specific demand for release of hostages, military withdrawal, or other political objective. The most recent wave of religion-based terrorism is accompanied by such demands as withdrawing U.S. troops from Saudi Arabia or the end of U.S. support for Israel. Even the Unabomber, widely regarded as a loner, had a remote political agenda for saving American society from the devastating influences of advanced technology.

In most cases the political demands of terrorists do not generate concessions, yet there are enough successes to keep hopes alive. The targeting of American and French citizens in Lebanon contributed to the decisions of those countries to withdraw their forces from Lebanon. Hezbollah (the Party of God) is generally regarded in Lebanon as the successful vanquisher of the Israeli occupation. Eighteen months after the slaughter of the Israeli athletes in Munich, Yasser Arafat was invited to address the UN General Assembly. Hope for terrorists is also kept alive by the prospect that minorities within enemy countries may constitute a political force favoring terrorism (Crenshaw, 1997: 154-155):

> In some cases, the support [for terrorism] is linked to ethnic or ethnonationalist divisions within a society that leave a minority community feeling threatened by a majority community, or seeking a separate solution. In Western democracies, we think immediately of Ireland and the IRA; Spain and the Basque population; and also France and the Corsicans. . . .[E]ven in liberal democracies with no significant social cleavages, terrorist underground movements may enjoy a reasonable amount of social support, enough to hamper a government response.

World Opinion

One kind of dialogue between terrorists and their enemy societies is the contest that is carried out before a final kind of audience, which can be called, for want of a better term, the *audience of world opinion*. Both terrorists and their target nations vie for attention and legitimacy before this partly real and partly imagined audience. In many respects the struggle is a symbolic game of last tag—the attempt on both sides to place themselves forward in world opinion as being the righteous victim and the other party as the aggressor. This kind of contest is a familiar one; protestors and police forces constantly engage in the struggle to avoid being tagged with the labels of unprovoked aggression, excess, and illegitimacy. Even though outcomes are never certain in the audience of world opinion, the imagined consequences of winning or losing are significant, and the impulse to compete in this arena remains alive.

Audiences in Perspective

With respect to the possibilities of deterring terrorism, each of these several audiences has a different status. The *supply of recruits* and the effectiveness of terrorist organizations in recruiting them are not easy to control in the short run, except for a conceivable modest impact that infiltrators and agents may have on recruitment strategies. In the longer run, affecting the educational systems and fostering appropriate economic and social changes in the countries of origin of terrorism, attempting to work with nations' leaders on successfully containing and controlling terrorists, and enlightened foreign policies on the part of the United States can affect the supply of alienated and potentially interested terrorists. The *attention-getting* characteristics of terrorists—especially leaders—are by and large beyond any kind of meaningful intervention. It is possible that the mass media could develop voluntary understandings among themselves to limit sensationalism in reporting terrorist events. Also essentially beyond outside control are the *internal dynamics* of how terrorists communicate with one another, except, again, for the modest impact that surveillance and infiltrators may have. *Audiences in host countries* can be affected mainly by the policies of those regimes in fostering economic and social stability and in not alienating their own populations through political repression; the United States can have a role in these processes by working with those regimes. Finally, with respect to *audiences in the United States* and *world public opinion*, this appears to be an ongoing process involving enlightened political policies on the part of the United States—and communicating them effectively—and engaging as effectively as possible in the inevitable game of last tag mentioned earlier (Hoffman, 1998; Lewis, 2002; Pillar, 2001).

Two hopeful notes with respect to audience effect should be mentioned. First, because the audiences for terrorists are multiple, they run the risk of pleasing one and alienating another by the same action; this creates public relations problems for them. Second, far from being completely steadfast and resolute, terrorists are driven by the need for action and audience support, and long periods of time between actions make for restlessness, feelings of isolation and entrapment, and a heightened tendency for internal conflicts over means and ends (Kellen, 1979). Policies of patience and containment on multiple fronts may encourage impatience in terrorist organizations and a waning of interest in their relevant audiences. The ingredients of such policies would include (a) containing terrorist organizations militarily, (b) destroying them when necessary, (c) securing U.S. borders, (d) making targets as inaccessible as possible; (e) supporting alternative ideologies, and (f) working deliberately with third parties who can possibly neutralize terrorist activities. This combination constitutes perhaps the most conducive set of conditions for the stagnation, withering, burnout, and eventual natural death of terrorist groups (Gurr, 1998).

ORGANIZATION OF TERRORIST NETWORKS

The preferred organizational form for terrorism is networks or, perhaps better, networks of network-based organizations (Arquilla and Ronfeldt, 2001). As such they are—like other aspects of terrorism—relatively unfamiliar to those who study organizations, who have focused more on formal organizations, such as corporations, hospitals, universities, civil service bureaucracies, voluntary organizations, and organizations developed to direct the activities of social movements. As a result, there are only some, mainly indirect insights about terrorist organizations from the literature on formal organizations.

The characteristics of terrorist organizations can be understood by tracing out the implications of the fact that terrorism must be simultaneously invisible and at the same time coordinated for preparing and executing terrorist activities. Consistent with these purposes, terrorist organizations must maintain extreme secrecy, avoid record keeping, and minimize any paper trails that could reveal their internal movements, plans, and intentions. The last is extremely difficult to ensure completely, because of the necessity to rely on computer and telephone—in addition to handwritten and face-to-face—communication as a part of organizational coordination, and the necessity sometimes to rely on financial transaction institutions to shift resources from place to place and on credit cards to facilitate movements of their personnel by cars, buses, trains, and airplanes.

The foreign affairs or external political exigencies of terrorist organizations are limited and concern mainly their relations with the host states in which they are located. If they are unknown to those states—rarely if ever the case—then questions of foreign relations with them are moot, because terrorist organizations avoid routine interactions with governing regimes. However, host states usually know about, tolerate, protect, or promote terrorist organizations for their own political purposes. This knowledge means establishing relations with terrorist organizations, taking an interest in and perhaps influencing their activities, thus forcing the terrorist organizations to observe and perhaps play along with various state-related realities.

Because much of the glue of contemporary terrorist organizations is commitment to an extreme ideology, there is a special range of issues of maintaining internal control. They must recruit those whom they regard as ideologically committed and ideologically correct. They must dedicate some of their organizational activities to maintaining that loyalty and commitment and preventing backsliding among members who are frequently living in societies with values, ways of life, and institutions that are different from their own and may be found seductive. The need to maintain various kinds of discipline through intense personal ties, hierarchical control, and surveillance is very strong. Organizations have to ensure that information flows but also that information is kept secret. They may have to coordinate extremely complex activities of destruction. And they must attend to the steadiness of ideological commitment.

There are several associated points of vulnerability of terrorist organizations, many of which involve failures of information flow, security of information, and coordination of activities. Organizations may also be subject to internal rivalries among leaders, especially if they are only partially integrated as networks of organizations. One additional vulnerability, characteristic of all ideologically extreme organizations, is the constant danger of schismatic ideological tendencies from within. Demanding extreme conformity, such organizations constantly face problems of internal deviation, mutual accusations among both leaders and followers that they are less than true believers, the splitting off of factions based on ideological differences, and the political intrigues that are involved in preventing such splits and dealing with them once they occur.

Direct knowledge about these organizational dynamics is

very limited, mainly because it is so difficult to study organizations that are bent on secret operations and concealment of information. Such knowledge must usually come from electronic surveillance, defectors, detainees who cooperate, and agents who have been able to infiltrate. However, the world has experienced many other kinds of secret, network-based organizations, and a base of knowledge about them and their operations has accumulated. Among these organizations are spy networks, gang rings such as the Mafia, drug-trafficking organizations, Communist cells, sabotage operations undertaken during wartime and during the cold war period, and extremist social and political movement organizations. In addition, network analysis as a field of study in sociology, social psychology, and elsewhere has yielded a great deal of theoretical and empirical knowledge during recent decades, and some aspects of this general knowledge might also be brought to bear.

We conclude this section on motives, values, and organization of terrorist organizations by noting a number of potential limitations on and vulnerability of contemporary terrorism: (a) their partial dependence on "domestic" friendly audiences, whose support and applause can wane if the terrorists appear to be inept or gratuitously excessive in their activities (Gurr, 1998; Crenshaw, 1999; Wieviorka, 1993; Post, 2001); (b) their dependence on states within which they operate—variable in terms of their precise relationship with those states—which may constrain their activities in light of their own "state" interests in the international arena; (c) extreme ideological and religious rigidity and backsliding, both of which have the potential to generate schisms within the terrorist organizations; (d) motivational failings, reversals, and defections, always a possibility when so much psychic energy is invested in an extreme cause; and (e) organizational failures, especially flows of information in a dispersed, secretive network.

CONDITIONS AND CONTEXTS OF TERRORISM

We now move to a more general level of analysis: to conditions fostering the rise of terrorism and the social, political, and cultural contexts in which it develops. To consider this is to leave the realm of deterrence in the short run and to move to more indeterminate background conditions. We continue to focus on the problems of prevention, though in the longer run.

HISTORICAL GIVENS OF CONTEMPORARY TERRORISM

Before moving to demographic, economic, and social conditions, we mention three broad contextual features of contemporary terrorism. None of these features concerns policy areas— that is, things one can or wants to do something about—but they constitute the broadest possible contexts for understanding terrorism as a historical phenomenon.

The first consideration concerns terrorism as a form of conflict. Throughout most of human history, warfare has been a form of conflict undertaken by two or more parties (tribes, regions, nations), each of which operates under the belief—not necessarily based on adequate information—that it has a chance of vanquishing the other by available military means. This might be called the assumption of imagined parity. That assumption is still roughly valid for many local wars throughout the world, but the larger picture has changed radically with the advent of weapons of mass destruction and a new asymmetry between the strong and weak nations of the world. During the cold war, there were two superpowers with weaponry capable of destroying one another and perhaps the rest of the world. The Soviet Empire and the Western Alliance engaged in a standoff of mutual deterrence during those four decades and relied on other means—diplomacy, propaganda, economic aid, clandestine international strategies of political disruption, and limited wars—in other parts of the world.

With the collapse of the Soviet Union in 1989 and its effective evaporation as a superpower, the United States—considered both alone and with its NATO allies—emerged as the sole superpower from a military point of view, with a quantum distance between it and the rest of the world. No country in the world can hope to challenge the United States militarily. No nation in the world can conceive of having the slimmest hope of winning a military war against the United States and its NATO allies. As a result, the options to wage conflict have narrowed. This situation has been fully in place for the past decade and continues; it may change if nuclear weapons and delivery technology proliferate sufficiently widely, but for the historical moment that is the dominant picture.

This general international situation reveals in large part why terrorism as a form of conflict has come into such prominence. It has emerged as a strategy of the enemies of the United States and the West in the context of their weakness, considered from a conventional military point of view. (Some beliefs, among them Muslim ones, hold that in the longer run God will prevail and victory will be achieved, or that the West, if disrupted, will collapse from the weight of its own corruption.) Terrorism as a system of harassing, disruptive, and destructive activities carried out by clandestine, stateless, mobile, and opportunistic networks of committed groups makes sense in this context of military imbalance. Such forms of violence are among the few options available. Considerations such as these give credence to the assessment that terrorism is a form of extortion from the strong by the weak.

The reason why contemporary terrorism is more than a nuisance is found in the second broad conditioning factor to be mentioned—technology. This factor is significant in two ways. First, the development of chemical, biological, and nuclear capabilities gives an enemy who can deploy them great destructive power. The potential willingness of terrorist organizations to use this technology wherever and whenever they can makes terrorism a real and present danger. Second, in U.S. and other developed societies, the deployment of technology in the interests of economic development and efficiency has created societies that are internally differentiated systems of interdependent parts. Crippling one sector—for example, the electrical system, the transportation system, the information technology system—quickly generalizes to other sectors, and as a result the entire system is vulnerable.

The third broad conditioning factor has to do with the increasing internationalization and interdependence of the world. This is often referred to with varying degrees of precision as globalization. To some degree, the idea of globalization has become an ingredient of terrorist and other ideologies, and it is represented as an extension of Western capitalism that disadvantages poorer countries. In another context, globalization has occasioned an extraordinary growth in the international movement of commodities, information, ideas, money, and people and, as a result, has necessarily increased the permeability of boundaries of society. This permeability makes all societies vulnerable to undetected penetration from outside, and terrorists can capitalize on this vulnerability. Regarded in this way, globalization constitutes an advantageous set of conditions for terrorists, both in terms of their capacity to locate in nonstate space and in their capacity to gain access to the societies of adversaries.

The reason we term these three conditions as "givens" is that they constitute the broad world historical context in which any efforts to prevent, contain, or disable terrorism must be developed.

POLITICAL CONSIDERATIONS

The political settings of terrorist activities during the past four decades have been dispersed and complex, and for that reason they defy simple generalizations. The areas of operation of terrorists during this period include dozens of countries and regions. Their political/ideological motivations include nationalism, separatism, both right- and left-wing radical, revolutionary, and Islamist beliefs. Many terrorist groups have only local horizons, many others have international missions, and still others have a mix of both. No single political formula applies to this scene of great diversity—though anticapitalism, antiimperialism, and antimodernity themes are frequent—and, correspondingly, no simple political formula for dealing with them emerges. In fact, a recent exhaustive survey of counterterrorist activities undertaken by the United States includes "negotiation of international agreements, military strikes against state sponsors of terrorism, and the creation of decontamination teams, changes in immigration procedures, advances in surveillance, and an increase in the severity of penalties associated with terrorist attack" (Donahue, 2001: 2). In light of this great historical diversity, however measured, the first lesson to be learned about political responses to terrorism is that a certain ad hoc and flexible approach is necessary and desirable.

Some words can be said on the politics of terrorist activities that command the most immediate attention—those associated with radical Islamic fundamentalism—though these are only a part of the whole terrorist picture. It is well known that these groups target unbelief as their main enemy, and this includes both Western countries and local, secularizing political regimes with an interest in modernizing their countries. In the twentieth centuries, nationalist elites, usually secular, either captured power (Turkey, Indonesia, Egypt, Pakistan, for example) or allied themselves with modernizing monarchies (Afghanistan, Iran).

These regimes were often opposed—sometimes quietly, sometimes noisily—by the traditional religious hierarchies. The most active opposition took the form of demanding an Islam-based state (the Muslim Brotherhood in Egypt, the Pakistani Islamic Party, and the Dar ul Islam movement in Indonesia). State policies toward these religious movements varied between toleration and brutal repression (especially of the more radical movements). Correspondingly, some of the movements worked themselves into the polity as lobbies or opposition parties, and some of them were driven underground and became even more radicalized in their religious and political outlook, developing a more systematic view of what an Islamic state or the Islamic community should be and more intolerant of anything that deviated from that. Included in the ideology of these groups was a thoroughgoing hatred of the military power of the West. It comes as no surprise that radical Islam is one of the feeder sources to anti-Western terrorism.

The policy of state repression has been as often counterproductive as it has been effective. As indicated, repression drives movements underground and tends to radicalize them. It may also drive movements out of the country to more hospitable environments. In addition, imprisonment of leaders and others often leads to the use of the prisons themselves as bases to breed radical ideas ("the best school for crime is a prison"). Repression also often radicalizes the repressive regime, which generalizes its fear of opposition to include more moderate forms, thus compromising the polity in an antidemocratic direction.

The lesson that emerges from this historical sketch is that the United States, in dealing with regimes in countries where terrorism has developed, ought to work as closely as it can with those regimes, but it should resist the temptation—strong as it is, because of the terrorist threat—simply to repress radical terrorist groups, because of the likely counterproductivity of simple and brutal repression (see Crenshaw, 1999; Post et al., 2002). The history of extremist groups in general indicates that a combined policy is preferable—repressing illegal and violent activities while simultaneously fashioning some kind of place in the political spectrum and the political process for both disaffected and moderate groups (Boulby, 1999; Wiktorowicz, 2001; Wickham, 1996). Neither radical political groups nor extremist religious organization are forever frozen in time as dangerous, destructive forces. To repress them as such—rather than recognizing that they have their own careers and are responsive to their political environments—does not remove them from the scene and may contribute to the very conditions in which they thrive (Shah-Kazemi, 1995; International Crisis Group, 2002; Chung, 2002; McDaniel, 1988; Auda, 1994).

DEMOGRAPHIC AND ECONOMIC CONSIDERATIONS

Because of the range and diversity of locations in which terrorism as an activity has developed, generalizations about demographic and economic origins are as difficult to come by as political generalizations, as are definitive long-term policies designed to deal with them. Nevertheless a few general observations can be made.

Terrorism is a strategy of the weak against the strong, and the broad array of terrorist activities in the past half-century gives broad credence to that view. The historical origins of the weakness of the weak are to be found in the centuries-long processes of differential economic development and disadvantage, colonization, the effects of wars and military domination—as the effects of these have accumulated.

Contemporary aspects of the weakness of nations outside the West include their demographic and economic disadvantages. Regarding Muslim states as a special case once again, we note that these countries are among those with the highest fertility rates in the world (though dropping in some places). This makes for not only rapid growth of their populations (a growth that itself places economic demands on those states), but also a particular age distribution of the population (many young, few old). The resulting youth dependency ratio puts great pressure on the education systems of these societies and also results in high proportions of young people in the economy who cannot find their way into paying and productive economic roles, and whose economic futures are dim (Kepel, 2002; United Nations Development Programme, 2002). The typical consequences of this situation are to generate great competitive pressures for marginal jobs domestically, pressures to emigrate, high unemployment among the young, and frequently large-scale social marginalization. Finally, a high growth ratio produces large numbers of children in families, and this may spread thin the family's financial and emotional resources. Some research (Sulloway, 1996; Skinner, 1992) suggests that later-born children in families are more rebellious. This research suggests the possibility that in a population in which many families have many children, the level of rebelliousness in the society may be higher than elsewhere.

The demographic sources of disadvantage combine with the economic realities that many of the Muslim nations are among the poor nations of the world, and that the distribution of wealth in them is among the most regressive (United Nations Development Programme, 2002). The origins of economic inequality lie both in the hierarchical traditions of these countries and in the fact that the fruits of mainly Western-induced economic development in them have not been distributed equitably. Both the demographic and the economic realities feed into high levels of social and political dissatisfaction in these nations, and when this dissatisfaction is given meaning in the context of anti-Western and radical Muslim ideologies, a fertile breeding ground for terrorist recruits is at hand (Guenena, 1986; Ibrahim, 1980, 2002; Dekmejian, 1995).

The demographic and economic disadvantages of these regions do not lend themselves to short-term cures, much less arenas for short-term deterrence of radical sentiments and terrorist activities. They are among the longer-term conditions. The longer-term picture is, however, that if these disadvantages persist in the political and religious contexts of this region, there is reason to believe that the social malaise, alienation, and disaffection of significant parts of the populations will also persist. Appreciating these realities does not provide neat formulas for what the long-term economic, political, and foreign policies of the United States and the West should be. They surely dictate, however, that those realities have to be taken into account if policies are to be enlightened.

CONCLUSION AND RECOMMENDATIONS

The one sure conclusion emerging from this report about strategies for countering terrorism is that there are no silver bullets or quick fixes available. It is possible to specify more effective and less effective deterrent and preventive policies at various levels and under different conditions. However, the general policy approach has to be adaptive, opportunistic, and multisided. The conventional problem-solving logic so attractive in American culture—find a problem and then fix it—is of limited utility, and a longer term, more contextualized approach is necessary.

Despite this important caution, the panel ventures the following specific recommendations about deterrence and prevention that follow from our analysis:

- Deterrence, understood conventionally as the direct use of threats, punishments, and inducements to prevent enemy action, has a viable place in dealing with terrorists.
- Many of the assumptions of conventional deterrence, however—availability of channels of communication, credibility among communicating parties, knowing what adversaries value—are not likely to be present in contemporary terrorist situations. As a result, reliance on direct deterrence can be only somewhat effective. In addition, direct threats and perceived overretaliation may have counterproductive effects with respect to generating support for terrorist groups and activities by uncommitted audiences.
- Direct efforts to deter should therefore be accompanied by working through all available third parties—societies hosting terrorist organizations, countries trusted by host societies, or the United States' own allies—who may have more credibility with and influence on terrorist organizations than this country, as enemy, does.
- Whenever possible, policies should be directed toward distancing and alienating relevant audiences from terrorist organizations and activities. The incorporation of potentially extremist political groups into the civil society of actual and potential host societies is especially important.

• Intelligence, infiltration, and related activities should be directed at points of vulnerability of terrorist organizations—their reliance on audience, their ideological inflexibility, their problems of maintaining commitments, and their potential for organizational failure.

• The social conditions fostering the rise of terrorism are complex and include demographic, economic, political, and educational factors. In the long run, preventive strategies should include improving these conditions in countries vulnerable to terrorist organizations and activities, as a means of diminishing the probabilities of their emergence and crystallization.

REFERENCES

Abootalebi, Ali R.
  1999 Islam, Islamists, and Democracy. [Online]. Available: http://meria.idc.ac.il/journal/1999/issue1/jvol3no1in.html [Accessed June 26, 2002].

Alam, Shah
  2000 Conservatives, Liberals and the Struggle Over Iranian Politics. [Online]. Available: http://www.ciaonet.org/olj/sa/sa_jun00als01.html [Accessed June 26, 2002].

Arquilla, John, and David Ronfeldt
  2001 *Networks and Netwars: The Future of Terror, Crime, and Militancy.* Santa Monica, CA: RAND.

Auda, Gehad
  1994 The "normalization" of the Islamic movement in Egypt from the 1970's to the early 1990's. In *Accounting for Fundamentalisms: The Dynamic Character of Movements,* M. Marty and R.S. Appleby (eds.). Chicago: University of Chicago Press.

Bandura, Albert
  1998 Mechanisms of moral disengagement. Pp. 161-191 in *Origins of Terrorism: Psychologies, Ideologies, Theologies, States of Mind,* Walter Reich (ed.). Washington, DC: Woodrow Wilson Center Press.

Boulby, Marion
  1999 *The Muslim Brotherhood and the Kings of Jordan, 1945-1993.* Atlanta: Scholars Press.

Chung, Chien-peng
  2002 China's "war on terror." *Foreign Affairs* 81(4): 8-12.

Crenshaw, Martha
  1997 Unintended consequences: How democracies respond to terrorism. *The Fletcher Forum of World Affairs,* 21:2, Summer/Fall:153-60.
  1999 How terrorism ends. Pp. 2-4 in *Special Report: How Terrorism Ends.* Washington, DC: U.S. Institute of Peace.

Dekmejian, R. Hrair
  1995 *Islam in Revolution: Fundamentalism in the Arab World.* 2nd ed. Syracuse, NY: Syracuse University Press.

Donahue, Laura K.
  2001 "In the Name of National Security: U.S. Counterterrorist Measures, 1960-2000." BCSIA Discussion Paper 2001-6, ESDP Discussion Paper ESDP-2001-04, John F. Kennedy School of Government, Harvard University.

Erickson, Bonnie
  1981 Secret societies and social structures. *Social Forces* 60(1):188-210

Ferracuti, Franco
  1998 Ideology and repentance: Terrorism in Italy. Pp. 59-64 in *Origins of Terrorism: Psychologies, Ideologies, Theologies, States of Mind,* Walter Reich (ed.) Washington, DC: Woodrow Wilson Center Press.

Guenena, Nemat
  1986 The "Jihad": An Islamic alternative in Egypt. *Cairo Papers in Social Science,* Vol. 9, Monograph 2 (Summer).

Gurr, Ted
    1998   Terrorism in democracies: Its social and political bases. Pp. 86-102 in *Origins of Terrorism: Psychologies, Ideologies, Theologies, States of Mind,* Walter Reich (ed.). Washington, DC: Woodrow Wilson Center Press.

Hamzeh, A. Nizar
    1997   Islamism in Lebanon: A Guide. [Online]. Available: http://meria.idc.ac.il/journal/1997/issue3/jvol1no3in.html [Accessed June 26, 2002].

Hoffman, Bruce
    1998   *Inside Terrorism.* New York: Columbia University Press.
    2001   All you need is love. *Atlantic Monthly* [Online]. Available: http://www.theatlantic.com/issues/2001/12/hoffman.htm [Accessed February 13, 2002].

Ibrahim, Saad Eddin
    1980   Anatomy of Egypt's militant Islamic groups: Methodological note and preliminary findings. *International Journal of Middle East Studies* 12(4):423-453 (December).
    2002   *Egypt, Islam, and Democracy.* Cairo, Egypt: American University in Cairo Press.

International Crisis Group
    2002   The IMU and the Hizb-ut-Tahir: Implications of the Afghanistan Campaign. ICG Asia Briefing Paper, Osh/Brussels, 30 January.

Kellen, Konrad
    1979   *Terrorists—What are They Like? How Some Terrorists Describe Their World and Actions.* Santa Monica, CA: RAND.

Kepel, Gilles
    2002   *Jihad: The trail of political Islam.* Cambridge, MA: Harvard University Press.

Kleiman, Mark A.R.
    1992   *Against Excess: Drug Policy for Results.* New York: Basic Books.

Krueger, Alan and Jitka Maleckova
    2002   Does poverty cause terrorism? *New Republic* 226(24):27-34.

Lewis, Bernard
    2002   *What Went Wrong? Western Impact and Middle Eastern Response.* Oxford, England: Oxford University Press.

Library of Congress
    1999   *The Sociology and Psychology of Terrorism: Who Becomes a Terrorist and Why?* Report prepared under an interagency agreement by the Federal Research Division, Hudson, Rex. Washington, DC: Library of Congress. [Online]. Available: http://www.loc.gov/rr/frd/Sociology-Psychology%20of%20Terrorism.htm [Accessed: June 26, 2002]

Lofland, John
    1966   *Doomsday Cult: A Study of Conversion, Proselytization, and Maintenance of Faith.* Englewood Cliffs, NJ: Prentice-Hall.

Maddy-Weitzman, Bruce
    1996   The Islamic challenge in North Africa. *Terrorism and Political Violence* 8(2):171-188 (Summer).

McCauley, Clark
    In   Psychological issues in understanding terrorism and the response to press terrorism in *The Psychology of Terrorism,* Christopher Stout (ed.). Westport, CT: Greenwood Publishing.

2002 Understanding the 9/11 perpetrators: Crazy, lost in hate, or martyred? In *History Behind the Headlines*, Vol. 5, N. Matuszak (ed.). Farmington Hills, MI: Gale Publishing Group.

McDaniel, Timothy
1988 *Autocracy, Capitalism, and Revolution in Russia.* Berkeley, CA: University of California Press.

Nagin, Daniel S.
1998 Criminal deterrence research at the outset of the twenty-first century. *Crime and Justice: A Review of Research* 23:1-42.

National Research Council
2002 *Making the Nation Safer: The Role of Science and Technology in Countering Terrorism.* Committee on Science and Technology for Countering Terrorism. Washington, DC: National Academy Press.
In *Terrorism: Perspectives from the Behavioral and Social Sciences.* Neil
press Smelser and Faith Mitchell, eds. Panel on Behavioral, Social, and Institutional Issues. Washington, DC: National Academy Press.

Pape, Robert A.
1996 *Bombing to Win.* Ithaca, NY: Cornell University Press.

Pillar, Paul R.
2001 *Terrorism and U.S. Foreign Policy.* Washington, DC: Brookings Institute Press.

Pollack, Kenneth
2001 Anti-Americanism and the Roots of Middle Eastern Terrorism. Working paper, Council on Foreign Relations, online at: http://www.ciaonet.org/newfrm.html [Accessed, Aug. 13, 2002].

Post, Jerrold M.
1998 Terrorist psycho-logic: Terrorist behavior as a product of psychological forces. Pp. 25-40 in *Origins of Terrorism: Psychologies, Theologies, States of Mind,* Walter Reich (ed.). Washington, DC: Woodrow Wilson Center Press.
2001 The Mind of the Terrorist: Individual and Group Psychology of Terrorist Behavior. Testimony prepared for Subcommittee on Emerging Threats and Capabilities, Senate Armed Services Committee, Nov. 15, 2001.

Post, Jerrold M., Keven G. Ruby, and Eric D. Shaw
2002 The radical group in context: 1. An integrated framework for the analysis of group risk for terrorism. *Studies in Conflict and Terrorism* 25(2):73-100

Schelling, Thomas C.
1984 *Choice and Consequence.* Cambridge, MA: Harvard University Press.
1966 *Arms and Influence.* New Haven, CT: Yale University Press.

Schmid, Alex P., A.J. Jongman, M. Stohl
1988 *Political Terrorism: A New Guide to Actors, Authors, Concepts, Data Bases, Theories and Literature.* New Brunswick, NJ: Transaction Books.

Shah-Kazemi, Reza
1995 *Crisis in Chechnia: Russian Imperialism, Chechen Nationalism, Militant Sufism.* London: Islamic World Report.

Shuja, Sharif
2001 Islam and the West: From discord to understanding. *Contemporary Review* 278:257-263.

Sivan, Emmanuel

    1997   Why Radical Muslims Aren't Taking Over Governments. [Online]. Available: http://www.meforum.org/meq/dec97/toc.shtml [Accessed June 26, 2002].

Skinner, G.W.

    1992   Family Process and Political Process in Modern Chinese History. Seek a Loyal Subject in a Filial Son: Family Roots of Political Orientation in Chinese Society. Sponsored by the Institute of Modern History, Academia Sinica; Department of History, University of California, Davis; Chian Ching-kuo Foundation for International Scholarly Exchange, Taipeh, Republic of China.

Snow, David, E.B. Rochford, Jr., S. Worden, and R. Benford

    1986   Frame alignment processes, micromobilization, and movement participation. *American Sociological Review* 51:464-481.

Sprinzak, Ehud

    1998   *From Theory to Practice: Developing Early Warning Indicators for Terrorism.* Washington, DC: U.S. Institute of Peace.

    2001   The lone gunmen: The global war on terrorism faces a new brand of enemy. *Foreign Policy* 127:72-73.

Stout, Christopher (ed.)

    In   *The Psychology of Terrorism.* Westport CT: Greenwood Press.
    press

Sulloway, Frank

    1996   *Born to Rebel.* New York: Pantheon.

United Nations Development Programme

    2002   Arab Human Development Report 2002. [Online] Available: http://www.undp.org/ [Accessed July 18, 2002].

Wickham, Carrie R.

    1996   Islamic mobilization and political change: The Islamic trend in Egypt's professional associations. Pp.120-135 in *Political Islam,* J. Beinin and J. Stork (eds.). Berkeley: University of California Press.

Wieviorka, Michel

    1993   *The Making of Terrorism,* translated by D.G. White. Chicago: University of Chicago Press.

Wiktorowicz, Quintan

    2001   *The Management of Islamic Activism: Salafis, the Muslim Brotherhood, and State Power in Jordan.* Albany: State University of New York Press.

Winner, Andrew C.

    2002   *Coalitions and Coercive Diplomacy,* dissertation accepted by the Department of Government and Politics, University of Maryland.